INFERNO

THE DEVASTATING FIRESTORMS OF OCTOBER 1993
AS CHRONICLED BY THE STAFF OF THE ORANGE COUNTY REGISTER

AS THE FIRESTORM APPROACHES, A MANSION IN EMERALD BAY SEEMS TO CROUCH IN ANTICIPATION, SURROUNDED BY THE VEGETATION THAT GIVES THE EXCLUSIVE COMMUNITY ITS LUSH CHARACTER — AND POSES THE THREAT OF FIRE. PHOTO: CHAS METIVIER

Andrews and McMeel
A Universal Press Syndicate Company
Kansas City

INFERNO!

•

chapter I

THE GATHERING STORM

In the darkness of a windy night —
and of an arsonist's soul — a fire
erupts in Anaheim Hills and quickly
spreads. Firefighters defeat the
blazes — but know that conditions
promise greater struggles to come.
Page 9

•

chapter II

TRIAL BY FIRE

An arson-sparked fire quickly
threatens Laguna Beach. As Santa
Ana winds howl through the canyons,
the city lies helpless. Meanwhile, a
new fire springs to life
on Ortega Highway.
Page 21

•

chapter III

ASHES AND REBIRTH

A valiant stand by firefighters and a
miraculous shift in the wind stem the
fiery tide. As the embers cool,
Laguna's stunned residents take
stock and begin to reconstruct
their shattered lives.
Page 59

•

PROPELLED BY WINDS GUSTING TO 75 MPH, A WALL
OF FLAMES CRESTS THE HILL ABOVE THE EMERALD BAY
COMMUNITY. MOMENTS LATER IT WILL MAKE ITS
FINAL CHARGE TOWARD THE PACIFIC AND DOZENS OF
HOMES WILL BURN. PHOTO: BRUCE CHAMBERS

INFERNO!

Copyright ©1993 by The Orange County Register. All rights reserved. Printed in the United States of America. No part of this book may be used or reproduced in any manner whatsoever without written permission except in the case of reprints in the context of reviews.

For information, write Andrews and McMeel, a Universal Press Syndicate Company, 4900 Main Street, Kansas City, Missouri 64112.
Library of Congress Catalog Card 93-74603
ISBN: 0-8362-8063-6

•

ATTENTION: SCHOOLS AND BUSINESSES

Andrews and McMeel books are available at quantity discounts with bulk purchase for educational, business or sales promotional use. For information, please write to: Special Sales Department, Andrews and McMeel, 4900 Main Street, Kansas City, Missouri 64112.

•

STAFF

This book is the collaborative effort of The Orange County Register news staff. It was edited and written by Richard E. Cheverton. Designed by Brenda Shoun. Photo-edited by Ron Londen and Chris Carlson. Cyber-edited by Val Cohen. Copy-edited by Marilyn Iturri. Part of the proceeds will be donated to fire recovery programs. The Register gratefully acknowledges the efforts of its staff and those of South County News and North County News, which made this book and the contribution to fire relief possible.

COVER PHOTO BY CHAS METIVIER

A HOUSE IN LAGUNA BEACH IS ATTACKED BY THE RELENTLESS WIND-WHIPPED FLAMES AS FIREFIGHTERS MAKE A VALIANT EFFORT TO STAVE OFF FATE. WHILE 366 STRUCTURES BURNED, FIREFIGHTERS MANAGED TO SAVE OVER A THOUSAND MORE. PHOTO: CHAS METIVIER

FROM THE EDITOR

Never before has Orange County faced a disaster the magnitude of these October 1993 firestorms. The photographs and words that follow are powerful and riveting — but they are only a glimpse, really, of the lightning ferocity of an event that left hundreds of homes and thousands of acres of pristine canyon land reduced to ashes.

It was a disaster that touched thousands of lives, often in quixotic, unpredictable ways. Many associates here at The Orange County Register were directly affected by the fire — it wasn't a story we reported; it was one we *lived*.

I will never forget watching the story unfold, filled with admiration at the remarkable job done at considerable personal risk by our staff; but also filled with fear that the home I had just moved into in Laguna would burn. I later learned that three neighbors whom I hardly knew had stayed after the official call for evacuation to train their garden hoses on my roof.

That act of heroism was repeated hundreds, probably thousands of times during the firestorm by private citizens and firefighters alike. In Laguna and Emerald Bay. In Villa Park and the El Morro mobile home park. Along the Ortega Highway. These acts of courage are the true legacy of this fire.

Yes, there were thousands of acres burned, hundreds of homes destroyed, uncountable possessions turned into ash.

But long after our lives return to normal — as they surely will — we will remember these triumphs of human compassion, large and small. And we will remember not the tears, but the courage and spirit of a community that was tested and tempered — forged, strong and new — by fire.

Tonnie L. Katz

TONNIE L. KATZ

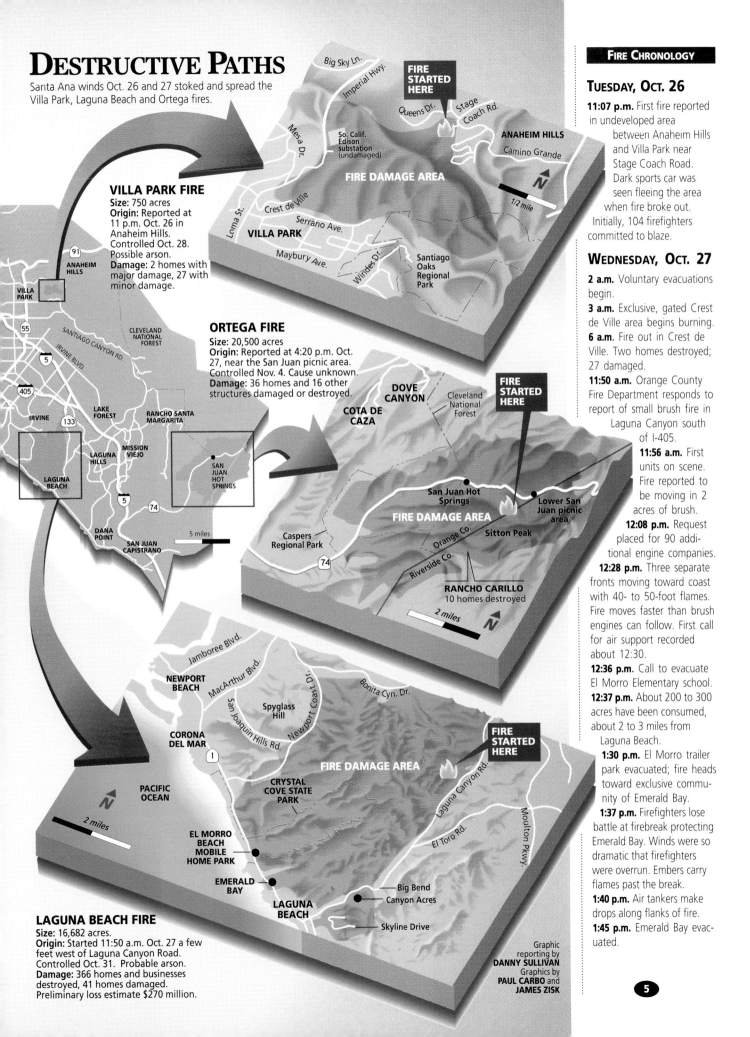

DESTRUCTIVE PATHS

Santa Ana winds Oct. 26 and 27 stoked and spread the Villa Park, Laguna Beach and Ortega fires.

FIRE STARTED HERE

ANAHEIM HILLS

Big Sky Ln.

Imperial Hwy.

Queens Dr.

Stage Coach Rd.

Camino Grande

So. Calif. Edison substation (undamaged)

Mesa Dr.

FIRE DAMAGE AREA

1/2 mile

VILLA PARK FIRE
Size: 750 acres
Origin: Reported at 11 p.m. Oct. 26 in Anaheim Hills. Controlled Oct. 28. Possible arson.
Damage: 2 homes with major damage, 27 with minor damage.

Loma St.
Crest de Ville
Serrano Ave.
VILLA PARK
Maybury Ave.
Windes Dr.
Santiago Oaks Regional Park

91
ANAHEIM HILLS
VILLA PARK
55
SANTIAGO CANYON RD.
CLEVELAND NATIONAL FOREST
IRVINE BLVD.
5
405
IRVINE
133
LAKE FOREST
RANCHO SANTA MARGARITA
LAGUNA HILLS
MISSION VIEJO
SAN JUAN HOT SPRINGS
LAGUNA BEACH
5
74
DANA POINT
SAN JUAN CAPISTRANO

5 miles

ORTEGA FIRE
Size: 20,500 acres
Origin: Reported at 4:20 p.m. Oct. 27, near the San Juan picnic area. Controlled Nov. 4. Cause unknown.
Damage: 36 homes and 16 other structures damaged or destroyed.

DOVE CANYON
COTA DE CAZA
Cleveland National Forest
FIRE STARTED HERE
San Juan Hot Springs
Lower San Juan picnic area
FIRE DAMAGE AREA
Caspers Regional Park
Orange Co.
Sitton Peak
Riverside Co.
74
RANCHO CARILLO
10 homes destroyed

2 miles

Jamboree Blvd.
NEWPORT BEACH
MacArthur Blvd.
Bonita Cyn. Dr.
Newport Coast Dr.
Spyglass Hill
San Joaquin Hills Rd.
CORONA DEL MAR
1
FIRE STARTED HERE
PACIFIC OCEAN
FIRE DAMAGE AREA
Laguna Canyon Rd.
2 miles
CRYSTAL COVE STATE PARK
Moulton Pkwy.
EL MORRO BEACH MOBILE HOME PARK
El Toro Rd.
EMERALD BAY
Big Bend
Canyon Acres
LAGUNA BEACH
Skyline Drive

LAGUNA BEACH FIRE
Size: 16,682 acres.
Origin: Started 11:50 a.m. Oct. 27 a few feet west of Laguna Canyon Road. Controlled Oct. 31. Probable arson.
Damage: 366 homes and businesses destroyed, 41 homes damaged. Preliminary loss estimate $270 million.

Graphic reporting by
DANNY SULLIVAN
Graphics by
PAUL CARBO and
JAMES ZISK

TUESDAY, OCT. 26

11:07 p.m. First fire reported in undeveloped area between Anaheim Hills and Villa Park near Stage Coach Road. Dark sports car was seen fleeing the area when fire broke out. Initially, 104 firefighters committed to blaze.

WEDNESDAY, OCT. 27

2 a.m. Voluntary evacuations begin.
3 a.m. Exclusive, gated Crest de Ville area begins burning.
6 a.m. Fire out in Crest de Ville. Two homes destroyed; 27 damaged.
11:50 a.m. Orange County Fire Department responds to report of small brush fire in Laguna Canyon south of I-405.
11:56 a.m. First units on scene. Fire reported to be moving in 2 acres of brush.
12:08 p.m. Request placed for 90 additional engine companies.
12:28 p.m. Three separate fronts moving toward coast with 40- to 50-foot flames. Fire moves faster than brush engines can follow. First call for air support recorded about 12:30.
12:36 p.m. Call to evacuate El Morro Elementary school.
12:37 p.m. About 200 to 300 acres have been consumed, about 2 to 3 miles from Laguna Beach.
1:30 p.m. El Morro trailer park evacuated; fire heads toward exclusive community of Emerald Bay.
1:37 p.m. Firefighters lose battle at firebreak protecting Emerald Bay. Winds were so dramatic that firefighters were overrun. Embers carry flames past the break.
1:40 p.m. Air tankers make drops along flanks of fire.
1:45 p.m. Emerald Bay evacuated.

2 p.m. Fire crests hills and sweeps toward north Laguna Beach. Meanwhile, a battle for Emerald Bay begins. Backfires are lit and sucked toward the main fire. Also, helicopters make spot drops near homes. However, embers set roofs afire. Flames spread from home to home, overwhelming fire-fighters. Firefighting contin-ues intensely for next hour and a half.

2:15 p.m. Fire sweeps down-Boat Canyon.

2:30 p.m. Fire's left flank burns toward Big Bend area. Backfires are set to save the Art Institute of Southern California.

2:45 p.m. Fire forces evacua-tion of the command center at El Morro Elementary school.

3 p.m. Fire jumps Laguna Canyon Road at Big Bend.

3:30 p.m. Fire on ridges all around Canyon Acres. Twenty engines diverted from Emerald Bay to protect hills east of Laguna Canyon Road.

3:55 p.m. Mandatory evacua-tion ordered in Canyon Acres; voluntary evacuation begins in the Mystic Hills area.

4 p.m. Crown Valley Parkway closed. Homes in Canyon Acres set afire when embers land on roofs. The few remaining residents fight the fires mostly alone, having been given a fire hose.

4:01 p.m. Downtown Laguna Beach ordered evacuated.

4:20 p.m. Three CH-53E choppers with water-carrying slings are on alert. Marines require a fire official to ride along; O.C. Fire Department says it doesn't have the manpower.

4:33 p.m. Command post at Thurston Intermediate School overrun by fire.

4:40 p.m. Flames approach Laguna Beach City Hall.

5:02 p.m. "Total gridlock" reported on Coast Highway.

THE COAST ABLAZE

The day was hot, and the wind was dry. Plants quickly gave up their moisture and became nothing more than kindling. When an arsonist set a fire in a small clearing near Laguna Lakes, the blaze took off dramatically toward the coast. It also spawned a smaller but terribly destructive fire that burned east of Laguna Canyon Road. At the end, fire had swept a path that consumed 366 buildings and 26 square miles of land.

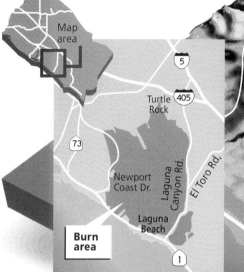

WESTERN PORTION

1 **Beginning of an inferno, 11:50 a.m.**

The first report of a small blaze came 10 minutes before noon. The first units to arrive found a football-field-sized area ablaze, and a request soon followed for 90 engines.

2 **Speeding to the coast, 12:30 p.m.**

Once flames escaped the valley of their origin, they flew along ridgelines toward the ocean with remarkable speed. Winds were blowing with gusts up to 78 mph. First call for air support was recorded about 12:30.

3 **Battle at Emerald Bay, 2 p.m**

Firefighters made a stand along a firebreak between urban areas and the wilderness. Flames were most intense at Emerald Bay, and firefighters were overrun at 1:30 p.m. By 2 p.m., embers ignited several roofs. A difficult battle raged for the next hour and a half to stop the fire's advance.

4 **El Morro next to fall, 5 p.m.**

Television showed dramatic footage of propane tanks exploding as the fire consumed an eastern portion of the El Morro Mobile Home Park. The majority of residents did not lose their homes, however, nor was the nearby elementary school damaged.

5 **Corona del Mar threatened, 7 p.m.**

With the onset of evening, a wind change occurred and the flames began moving toward the Newport Beach community of Corona del Mar. Between the flames and the homes stood Newport Coast Drive as a firebreak. Firefighters used it to their advantage, additionally cutting firelines in the brush with bulldozers.

6 **Turn toward Irvine, 8 p.m.**

Winds steered the flames more on a course toward Irvine Turtle Rock area. Some residents evacuated as the evening progressed. Around midnight, firefighters took advantage favorable winds to burn a large firebreak to protect the community. This left no fuel for the fire to consume, and t threat was ended.

A new fire begins, 3 p.m.

nd shift sent embers across Laguna Canyon Road,
e they ignited brush on a hillside. Flames moved
ly up the ridge and toward the heart of Laguna.

Canyon Acres succumbs, 3:30 p.m

surrounded the valley community of Canyon Acres and
ed quickly down the hillsides. There was virtually no
nse of the area, though resources were at this point
redeploying from Emerald Bay.

C Blaze hits Skyline, 4:30 p.m.

Flames rapidly climbed the hills toward homes on Skyline
Drive. Evacuees jammed roads to escape; there was little
warning of danger. Embers soon set houses ablaze. Even the
fire command post at Thurston Middle School was overrun.

D Taking a stand, 6 p.m.

Firefighters were massed to stop the flames. They were
hampered by continual losses of water pressure. Tankers
helped them keep flames from moving from the lower Park
Avenue area.

E Blaze contained, 3:30 a.m. Wednesday

The flames that started at Big Bend began moving
back around 8 p.m. Firefighters scrambled to cut a
fireline to keep the blaze from escaping.

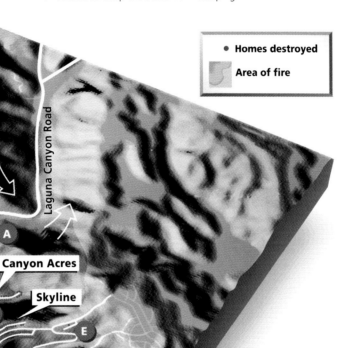

- ● **Homes destroyed**
- **Area of fire**

Emerald Canyon

Laguna Canyon Road

Canyon Acres

Skyline

Mystic Hills

Temple Hills

LAGUNA BEACH

Coast Highway (133)

N

Graphics reporting: DANNY SULLIVAN

Source: Orange County Fire Department, Laguna Beach Fire
Department, witnesses and news reports

Graphic: GEORGE TURNEY and JIM ZISK
The Orange County Register

THE FIRE'S TOLL

EMERALD BAY
Homes destroyed: 51
Damaged: 22

CANYON ACRES
Destroyed: 47
Damaged: 3

SKYLINE/ MYSTIC HILLS
Destroyed: 195
Damaged: 8

TEMPLE HILLS
Destroyed: 21

EL MORRO
MOBILE HOME PARK
Destroyed: 40
Damaged: 4

**Addresses of 12 other
destroyed buildings have
not yet been released.**

FIRE CHRONOLOGY

5:12 p.m. Traffic jam of
evacuees begins backing up
Temple Hills Drive.

5:17 p.m. Fire road is opened
to speed evacuation of people from the Top of the
World area.

5:27 p.m. Flames reported at
the rear of Laguna City Hall
and police station.

5:30 p.m. Flames moving
down through Mystic Hills
toward Thalia Street.
Firefighters make stand along
La Vista. Water pressure lost,
and firefighters nearly ready
to abandon street until tanker
and hoses from working
hydrant farther down allow
them to fight. Residents at far
end of street desperately beat
out flames with wet cloths
and even Coca-Cola.

6 p.m. Firefighters make a
stand below Temple Hills,
along lower Park Avenue.
They are helped by the burning neighborhoods to the
west. The heat creates a wind
that blocks the prevailing
Santa Anas, causing the fire
to move more slowly. Later, a
sea breeze with 60% to 70%
humidity moves in.

6:09 p.m. Order issued to
evacuate all of Laguna
Beach on the inland side of
Coast Highway, north of
Cress Street.

6:30 p.m. National Guard
says it has two heavy C-130
firefighting aircraft available
for use against Orange
County blazes, but they
have not been requested by
local officials.

8 p.m. Sea breeze pushes fire
into unburned bush surrounding Hidden Valley. Firefighters
work until 3:30 a.m. to keep
flames away from homes.

8:35 p.m. Irvine Police
Department asks for volun-
tary evacuation of Turtle
Rock area, between Ridge-
line Drive and Sierra Luna
Road.

9 p.m. New fire along Ortega Highway blackens 1,200 acres; structures are threatened.

11:25 p.m. Irvine Fire Department starts backfires on a line extending across the ridge just above Turtle Rock (Bonita Canyon).

THURSDAY, OCT. 28

1 a.m.: The threat of damage from the Ortega fire is greatly reduced by this time. After daybreak, heavy firefighting helicopters arrive to help battle the blaze.

3:30 a.m. Firefighters get line around last portion of fire east of Laguna Canyon Road. It was feared the fire might get over a ridge and into Bluebird Canyon. Meanwhile, fire officials say they will likely let Turtle Rock homeowners back into their homes soon.

4 a.m. Fire department spokesperson: "We're feeling very optimistic right now." The winds die down.

7:30 a.m. Fire officials declare Turtle Rock area safe, and they start letting residents back in.

6 p.m. Emerald Canyon fire declared contained.

FRIDAY, OCT. 29

The west flank of the Ortega fire is mostly surrounded by a firebreak. The east side continues raging, but only through wilderness where it threatens no homes.

MONDAY, NOV. 1

Firefighters have line completely surrounding Ortega fire.

WEDNESDAY, NOV. 3

Ortega fire declared controlled. Only isolated hot spots, well within burned areas, remain.

RIDGE WARFARE

At 3 p.m. Wednesday, the Emerald Canyon fire spread to two fronts when embers jumped across Laguna Canyon Road. Flames quickly decimated the communities of Canyon Acres, Skyline and Mystic Hills. Caught off guard, firefighters moved to keep flames pinned on the ridges west of Park Avenue. Residents who defied evacuation also battled the blazes any way possible.

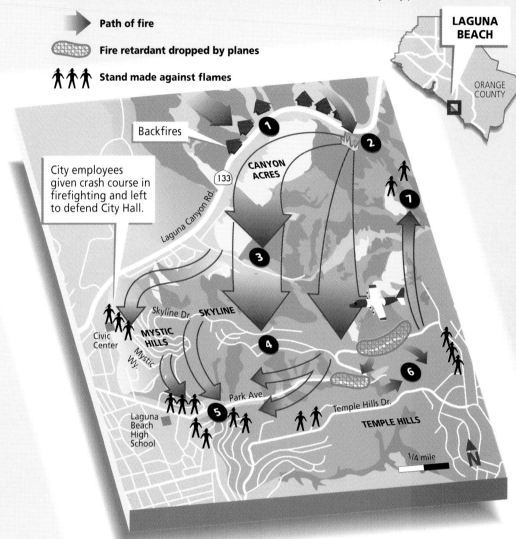

1 **Blaze approaches Big Bend, 2:30 p.m.**

Fire's left flank burns slowly toward Big Bend. Firefighters set backfires and save art school.

2 **Flames jump Laguna Canyon Road, 3 p.m.**

A strong wind shift blows embers across road, setting hillside on fire. Flames have quickly spread up ridge by the time firefighters arrive.

3 **Canyon Acres surrounded, 3:30 p.m**

Flames encircle the ridges above Canyon Acres, then creep down and destroy much of the neighborhood. The firestorm grows intense enough to suck the breath away from one who stayed.

4 **Skyline attacked, 4:30 p.m.**

Fire races up the ridge toward homes on Skyline Drive. Evacuations came only about a half-hour before. Embers blown by the strong wind quickly set the neighborhood on fire.

5 **Stand at Park Avenue, 6 p.m.**

Firefighters and residents fend off the flames, often hampered by a lack of water.

6 **Hidden Valley threatened, 8 p.m.**

A wind change that helped elsewhere sets unburned brush aflame around Hidden Valley. Firefighters work until 3:30 a.m. to keep flames away from buildings.

7 **End run averted, 3:30 a.m. Thursday**

The wind change also blows flames back toward Big Bend. Firefighters work feverishly to clear a line around the fire. This keeps flames from sweeping back toward Alta Laguna and Bluebird Canyon.

Graphics reporting : DANNY SULLIVAN

Source: Fire department reports and witness accounts

JAMES ZISK and GEORGE TURNEY
The Orange County Register

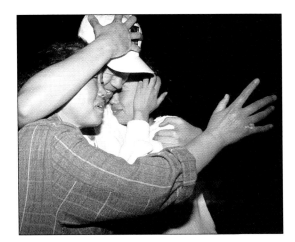

FIRST OF O.C. BLAZES A PORTENT OF DISASTER

The first fire in Orange County struck in Anaheim Hills late Tuesday and continued through Wednesday.

The blaze is similar to one that swept the area almost exactly 11 years ago, in October 1982, when 14 homes were destroyed and 17,000 acres scorched.

By Dan Froomkin
10/28/93

SANTA ANA WINDS FUEL DESTRUCTION

Twenty-five fire trucks lined the northeastern corner of upscale Villa Park; another 25 worked Orange Park Acres and the Orange foothills.

And 10 trucks were on the scene next to multimillion-dollar homes along Crest de Ville, an exclusive gated cul-de-sac that has been struck by wildfires twice in 30 years.

By James V. Grimaldi
10/28/93

> "WE FOUND KOI FISH IN A POND. WE FOUND LIVE GOLDFISH IN A BOWL, BUT, AS FULLY EXPECTED, WE DID NOT FIND ANY BODIES."
>
> Jim Beisner, deputy coroner Orange County

chapter I

GATHERING STORM

The chaparral waited for its ancient destiny. The exotic plants grafted onto the ephemeral Southern California ecology — eucalyptus, succulents, bougainvillea — baked in the opalescent October sun, awaiting its all-too-regular rendezvous with fire. In laboratories, worried men tracked the vegetation's moisture content, watching it plunge toward the critical 7-percent level, a number hardly noted by Orange County residents growing itchy and strangely irritable as the autumnal Santa Anas returned, as they always have; the first gusts coming in the night, the bone-dry winds leached of their moisture high over the howling Mojave desert; rushing now through canyon wind-tunnels — dead winds, carrying their freight of anger and the irrational.

Somewhere, somehow someone struck a match. That's all that was required to set the stage; the night's blowtorch winds took care of the rest. Caught by the the wind, it grew, like a genie released from a lamp, into a terrifying thing that rolled in waves of pure energy through the tinder-dry biomass — at first scattering screaming coyotes or startled hawks — then heading, as if drawn by some intelligence, into the world that humans had imposed on the ancient grasslands. Places named by stern German immigrants and real estate dreamers: Anaheim Hills, Villa Park, Crest de Ville. Places developed in good faith but with a bad sense of history's blackened record: homes planted smugly in ancient fire-chutes, in places that had burned — who knows how many times? — in an ecology founded on flame.

Now the flames had returned in a concentrated frenzy, churning into arabesques that were strangely liquid, awesome, beautiful and predatory.

Now the flames' enemy — brave firefighters in yellow slickers, reflective stripes glowing like wolf-eyes in the probing TV lights — interposed themselves. They had danced with the devil flames many times before; and even as they knocked down the blaze — crowding it, drenching it and tricking it with backfires — they must have sensed a portent: This was the season of fire and it would not be denied.

NEXT PAGE: AS THE WINDS HOWL AND EMBERS FILL THE SKY, FIREFIGHTERS HUNKER DOWN IN VILLA PARK EARLY WEDNESDAY.
PHOTO: DAVE YODER

FLAMES FORCE SURVIVAL SCRAMBLE

Wendy and Yudi Izenman, who moved to Dove Canyon last year from Los Angeles in the wake of the riots there, decided not to take any chances Wednesday.

"We don't know where we'll go. Maybe Disneyland Hotel and get some fun out of this," said Wendy Izenman, 40.

By Scott Duncan
10/28/93

"WHEN WE FIRST GOT HERE. THE FIRE WAS COMING UP THE BRUSH TWICE THE SIZE OF THE HOUSE."
Rene Garcia,
Anaheim fire captain

CANYON RESIDENTS MAKE QUICK RETREAT

A procession of Mercedes-Benzes, Ferraris and horse trailers poured out of Coto de Caza through the guard gate, and the manager of the equestrian center hurriedly contacted owners to retrieve their animals. About 90 of the 120 animals boarded there were removed by 8:30 p.m.

By Scott Duncan
10/28/93

THIS PAGE: FIREFIGHTERS RIP DOWN SHRUBBERY THREATENING TO TORCH A VILLA PARK HOUSE. BUT IT IS ALREADY BURNING.

NEXT PAGE: AS FIRE EATS AT THE NEIGHBORHOOD, NANCY STEMRICK OF VILLA PARK MAKES SOME OF THE FASTEST, TOUGHEST DECISIONS OF HER LIFE.
PHOTOS: DAVE YODER

13

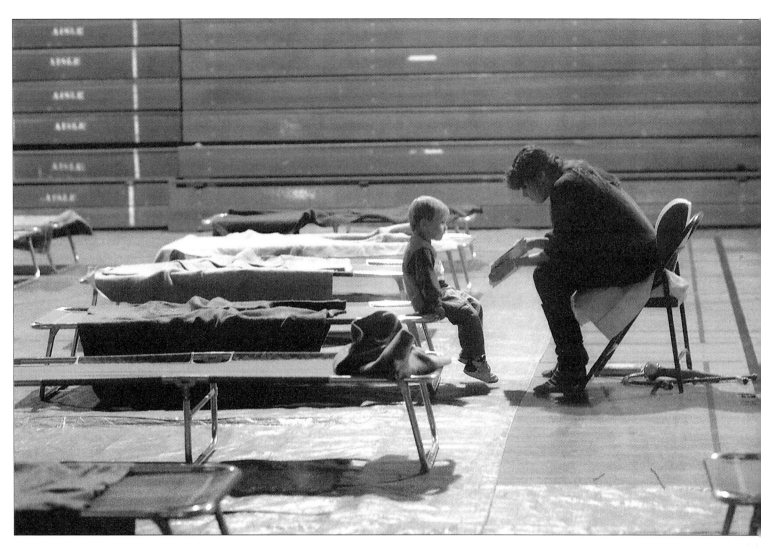

FAR LEFT: TREES LITERALLY
EXPLODE IN THE FIRE'S INTENSE
HEAT. **PHOTO: DAVE YODER**

TOP: AT A RED CROSS
EVACUATION CENTER AT VILLA
PARK HIGH SCHOOL, A BEDTIME
STORY IS SCANT COMFORT.
PHOTO: KEN STEINHARDT

LEFT: PURSUED BY FLAMES, NICK
STREMICK, 15, DASHES FOR
SAFETY IN VILLA PARK.
PHOTO: KEN STEINHARDT

TOP: STINGING EMBERS, HEAVY SMOKE SEND VILLA PARK POLICE OFFICERS REELING.
ABOVE: TEARS OF JOY AS PARK FAMILY MEMBERS REALIZE THEIR HOME HAS BEEN SAVED.

RIGHT: NOTHING TO DO BUT WAIT, WATCH AND HOPE. ROXANNE SOREL COMFORTS HER 9-YEAR-OLD
DAUGHTER, CONTESSA, AS FLAMES CRACKLE NEARBY. **PHOTOS: DAVE YODER**

As flames approach, firefighters fan out to make a stand. They succeeded; the Anaheim Hills house still stands. **Photo: Mark Avery**

chapter II

TRIAL BY FIRE

FROM THE REGISTER

WORST FIRE DISASTER IN COUNTY HISTORY

Monstrous firestorms propelled by devil's winds blasted Orange County on Wednesday, destroying more than 300 homes, incinerating more than 8,750 acres and forcing thousands of panicked evacuations in the county's worst fire-related disaster.

By Dan Froomkin
10/28/93

●

"THOSE TANKS WERE SHOOTING UP 200 FEET IN THE AIR LIKE MISSILES (AT EL MORRO TRAILER PARK). THEY CAN REPLACE THEIR HOMES; I CAN'T REPLACE MY FIREMEN."

Clinton Arnett,
El Toro Civilian Fire
Department

●

FRANTIC DASH TO SAVE FAMILY TREASURES

Joe Lademan, 25, tried to save his parents' Emerald Bay home by dousing the roof with a garden hose.

Speaking on a portable phone with his sister, Lademan received instructions on what valuables to save: pictures of his great grandparents, some jewelry, a family portrait. He grabbed what he could and ran for his life.

By Tracy Weber
and Jeordan Legon
10/28/93

NEXT PAGE: UNDER ITS FIERY CROWN, AN EMERALD BAY BUNGALOW REFLECTS ITS DEMISE IN POOLS OF USELESS WATER.
PHOTO: DANIEL A. ANDERSON

A t 11:56 a.m. Wednesday, October 27, 1993, the first Orange County fire trucks arrived at an unremarkable grass field, part of the vast Irvine Company landholdings; a field, in a sense, of dreams: fallow, waiting for recession's end and the developer's bulldozer. Here is where the most devastating fire in Orange County history began.

It was almost certainly started by an arsonist — an *au naturel* version of the drive-by shooter, a new arrival in the ecology of crime.

As the clock inched past high noon, nine acres fell; the flames lashing now, eager, almost yearning, heading off into the purple hills like bright pilgrims seeking salvation.

At 12:08, a request for 90 fire engines triggered a mutual aid response throughout the state. As fire department computers chattered silently to one another, the fire ate up the rolling bucolic hills — gnatcatcher country — and plunged into Laguna Canyon.

There it aimed a fiery dagger at the heart of the fascinating, contradictory village: home of corporate megamillionaires and unreconstructed hippies; free spirits and the design review board; art galleries and The Little Shrimp.

Now fire muscled into this adult dreamscape, gorging on the dense, picturesque hillsides, dancing giddily from shake roof to shake roof,

attacking El Morro's mobile homes and the rich, heavily guarded enclave of Emerald Bay with a terrifying rapaciousness that left residents united in terror.

As the fire bullied its way through the colony's narrow, twisting streets, individual acts of extraordinary heroism unfolded.

It was as capricious, as glorious, as war: Homeowners in flip-flops became Medal of Honor heroes; firefighters made valiant stands, then fell back.

Night fell. Still the flames cavorted like Halloween goblins, mocking 1,968 firefighters and 345 pieces of equipment.

Houses burst into flame in Technicolor explosions; Laguna had gone global on satellite dishes.

As the winds howled and danced, one thing seemed clear. Firefighters were in retreat — and only the Pacific Ocean would stop this monster.

PREVIOUS SPREAD: FIRE, THE GREAT EQUALIZER, FORCES TWO WOMEN TO FLEE ALLWYN DRIVE IN NORTH LAGUNA WITH THEIR PET CAT. **PHOTO: DON LEACH**

LEFT PAGE: BEACH SEATS.
PHOTO: LEONARD ORTIZ

THIS PAGE, TOP LEFT: AN AERIAL TANKER MAKES ITS HEART-STOPPING ATTACK.
PHOTO: BRUCE CHAMBERS

TOP RIGHT: BREA FIREMEN SURVEY THURSTON SCHOOL.
PHOTO: BRUCE STRONG

BELOW: A FIERY WAVE CRASHES AGAINST CANYON ROCKS.
PHOTO: LEONARD ORTIZ

'KUSTOM KULTURE' FACES THE FLAMES

The Laguna Art Museum closed at 1:30 p.m. so employees could stash the California art collection inside a fireproof vault. As the flames drew closer, and homes across the street were evacuated, curator Bolton Colton debated rolling custom-painted cars from the museum's "Kustom Kulture" show down the hill to the safety of the sand in Main Beach.

By Tracy Weber
and Jeordan Legon
10/28/93

"YOU COULD WALK FROM ONE CAR TO ANOTHER. IT'S JUST A STANDSTILL. IT'S HEADLIGHTS AS FAR AS YOU CAN SEE."

Ian Davis,
Laguna Beach resident

BEACH SPECTATORS WATCH THE CITY BURN

Hundreds of people waited at downtown Laguna's Main Beach. Dozens of stores shut down as customers and employees drifted onto the beach. They were joined by the curious, by the horrified, by those who could only watch helplessly as their homes or friends' homes began to be devoured by the blaze.

By Tracy Weber
and Jeordan Legon
10/28/93

STEVE FEATHER, A COSTA MESA FIREFIGHTER, BATTLES FLAMES, AND A FIREHOSE, IN AN ATTACK ON ROILING FLAMES IN EMERALD BAY.
PHOTO: CHAS METIVIER

29

FAR LEFT: LAGUNA RESIDENTS, SUCH AS SHANE SMITH, FOUGHT WITH WHATEVER WEAPONS WERE AT HAND — GARDEN HOSES, THEIR BARE HANDS — AS FLAMES ROARED CLOSER. **PHOTO: LEONARD ORTIZ**

LEFT: WHAT TO TAKE? WHAT TO LEAVE? LAGUNA RESIDENTS HAD SCANT MOMENTS TO DECIDE. KATE CARTLEDGE HELPS KIRSTEN BUCKLAND (LEFT) FLEE HER PINECREST DRIVE RESIDENCE, WHICH, IN THE END, WAS SPARED. **PHOTO: DANIEL A. ANDERSON**

BOTTOM: MARK POOLOUS WAS VISITING A FRIEND IN LAGUNA. SUDDENLY, HE WAS PRESSED INTO SERVICE TO DEFEAT THE ONRUSHING FIRE. **PHOTO: DON LEACH**

APOCALYPSE NOW FOR NATURE'S INNOCENTS

About 3 p.m. the sky black-ened into night, the sun burned a blood red and the streets overflowed with water, mud and fleeing wild animals.

It was the end of the world – their world.

By Tracy Weber
and Jeordan Legon
10/28/93

FROM THE AIR, AN ABSTRACT HORROR

A special Wescam camera system allowed KNBC-TV/4 pilots to get extra-close shots of Laguna Beach's flames. KNBC purchased the system after the Los Angeles riots "so we could cover dis-turbances safely," said Reed Manville, KNBC-TV presi-dent and general manager.

By Kinney Littlefield
10/28/93

PREVIOUS SPREAD: FIREFIGHTERS WORK TOGETHER IN DEADLY COMBAT.

THIS PAGE: LOW WATER PRESSURE – A MAJOR PROBLEM IN THE LAGUNA FIRE – DOESN'T DETER GREG KEARNS.

PHOTOS : BRUCE STRONG

WATCHING A REAL-LIFE HORROR SHOW

Out there, in Laguna Beach and Turtle Rock and Anaheim Hills, our world is a scarred and smoking hell. On television, safely contained within the box, the blaze seems as distant as a long-ago dream.

By Kinney Littlefield
10/29/93

ECLECTIC HEROES OF ST. ANNS DRIVE

They began with a prayer. Shouting above the approaching roar, Arthur recited the 23rd Psalm, improvising at one point: "Thy rod, thy staff and thy garden hose, they comfort me!" Baker added his own spiritual touch. As the hot winds blew around him, he solemnly performed a "wind dance" he hoped would make the Santa Ana winds shift in their favor.

Then they waited, hoses ready, wet towels tied around their noses and mouths.

By Martin J. Smith
10/29/93

> "AS YOU WATCH THE FLAMES, EACH ONE REACHING TO THE SKY. BENEATH THE BLANKET OF SMOKE IS YOUR PARENT'S HOUSE, BURNING TO THE GROUND. "
>
> Margalit Younger, 13, of Villa Park

LAGUNA RESIDENTS ROBERT AHLKE JR. (FRONT) AND BILL BALAIKA DEFY APPROACHING FLAMES TO DO WHATEVER THEY CAN TO SAVE THEIR HOME ON PINECREST DRIVE. THEY WON.
PHOTO: DANIEL A. ANDERSON

37

RIGHT PAGE: FIRE TAKES ITS LAST
SULLEN BITES OUT OF AN EMERALD
BAY NEIGHBORHOOD.
PHOTO: BRUCE CHAMBERS

THIS PAGE, RIGHT: BENEATH THE
SMOKE, AN UNREAL NIGHT
DESCENDS.
PHOTO: LEONARD ORTIZ

BELOW: NOTHING TO BE DONE.
FIRE IS VICTORIOUS — FOR NOW.
PHOTO: CHAS METIVIER

HIS HOME – THE ONE HE COULDN'T SAVE

One hour after a sooty dawn lifted over Skyline Drive in Laguna Beach, John and Barbara Lane saw what the darkness had veiled.

"There's nothing," Barbara Lane said, settling onto a cement step of what Wednesday was their home. "It melted everything. There's nothing to see."

John Lane stood calmly beside her in the yellow fire suit of the Orange County Fire Department. Even as he battled a fire near Rancho Santa Margarita on Wednesday, a swirling firestorm swallowed his home of 17 years.

By Tom Berg
10/29/93

LOOKING SKYWARD FOR A COUNTERATTACK

Helicopters circled overhead – Whap. Whap. Whap. – dumping water that sizzled in the heat. It was a war and Laguna was losing.

By Tracy Weber
and Jeordan Legon
10/28/93

PREVIOUS SPREAD: IN THE MIDST OF BATTLE, A FIREFIGHTER SPRAYS HIS TRUCK IN THE BLINDING HEAT.
PHOTO: JIM MAX

THIS PAGE: IT'S HOPELESS – LOS ALAMITOS FIRE CAPT. CRAIG AGOSTA WATCHES HELPLESSLY AS A LAGUNA HOUSE BURNS.
PHOTO: BRUCE STRONG

43

LEFT PAGE: BILL VALAIKA CHEERS
THE WATER-DROPPING CHOPPER
THAT SAVED HIS HOUSE.
PHOTO: DANIEL A. ANDERSON

THIS PAGE, TOP: A HOUSE BURNS
TO ITS TIMBER BONES.
PHOTO: MICHAEL GOULDING

LEFT: A TRAFFIC JAM OF FIRE
ENGINES MOVES TOWARD THE FIRE
FRONT IN EMERALD BAY.
PHOTO: BRUCE STRONG

FINDING A CITY BRUTALLY DISFIGURED

On Thursday morning I stood at the lip of Alta Laguna and saw a slice of hillside to the southwest, black and furry with burned grass. Here and there, the earth was chalked by ash; here and there it pouted smoke. A gray scrim of air blocked every tree and every home – those that were left. I couldn't see the ocean at all through the smoke.

To the northwest, the muted palette I loved was gone. Instead of chocolate-brown buckwheat, olive-colored trees and fat, yellow-green prickly pear, I saw charred ground and tree skeletons and prickly pear wizened in its new dark skin. A few clumps of ashy buckwheat stood tall, but most of the survivors were beer cans.

By Melissa Balmain
10/29/93

VIEWING THE FIRE FROM AFAR

Alone in a Stockholm hotel room, professional tennis player Rick Leach watched in disbelief as the fiery images flickered from the television screen.

"This is the worst feeling in the world. I'm sitting here recognizing houses in my neighborhood that are being burned down."

By Janis Carr
10/28/93

RIGHT: THE FIRESTORM TOOK AN ERRANT PATH THROUGH EMERALD BAY NEIGHBORHOODS, BURNING HOMES, LEAVING TREES AND OTHER BUILDINGS UNTOUCHED.
PHOTO: CHAS METIVIER

NEXT PAGE: FOR LAGUNA RESIDENT TOM MARSHALL, THERE WAS NOTHING TO DO BUT WAIT, AND WONDER.
PHOTO: MICHAEL KITADA

Far left: 'Ground-pounders' stand by as a backfire is started.
Photo: Dave Yoder

Top: Firefighter starts a fire to fight fire; it helped save Turtle Rock.
Photo: Robert Walchli

Left: Smudged, singed, unbowed; firefighter Joel Gonzalez traveled from the Crow Indian agency in Montana.
Photo: Lisa Romerein

WATER SHORTAGE ADDS TO DESTRUCTION

Miscues and political infighting by federal, state and local officials forced Orange County firefighters to battle one of the state's most disastrous wildfires with dangerously low water pressure and without help from water-dropping aircraft until it was too late.

By James V. Grimaldi
10/29/93

RUMORS SWIRL AS FIRE SPREADS

Hundreds of calls flooded the county's rumor-control hot line Thursday: Was the fire headed inland? Had the Little League baseball fields in Irvine burned? Was it true the Pacific Amphitheatre was charred?

No, no and no.

By Tracy Weber
and Jeordan Legon
10/29/93

> **"I'M SADDENED ABOUT THOSE WHO HAVE LOST THEIR HOMES. AS TO THE FIRE ON THE RANCH ITSELF, I'M FURTHER SADDENED THAT ENVIRONMENTALLY SENSITIVE LAND HAS IN SOME CASES BEEN DESTROYED BY FIRE."**
>
> **Donald Bren,
> Irvine Co. Chairman**

FIREFIGHTERS WATCH FOR DRIFTING EMBERS AS THE LAGUNA FIRE IS TURNED BACK.
PHOTO: LEONARD ORTIZ

LEFT: FIRE TRUCKS WAIT IN RESERVE ALONG COAST HIGHWAY, READY TO COMBAT HOT SPOTS.
PHOTO: NADIA BOROWSKI

ABOVE: THE RUINS OF EMERALD BAY.
PHOTO: BRUCE CHAMBERS

NEXT PAGE: MOONSCAPE. CORAL DRIVE FLOATS IN MOONLIGHT. **PHOTO: LEONARD ORTIZ**

FROM THE REGISTER

RESIDENTS STRUGGLE BACK TO LIFE

The day began with skies over Laguna Beach turning into an intense aerial ballet as news helicopters competed for morning-after shots.

Some lucky Laguna Beach residents awoke in their own homes and headed for spots such as Zinc Cafe on Ocean Avenue, drinking coffee they couldn't smell because the whole town had the stench of a barbecue gone bad.

By Marilyn Kalfus
10/29/93

> **"THINGS NOW ARE VERY NORMAL AND VERY ABNORMAL."**
> **William Cavenaugh, Laguna Beach police captain**

CURIOSITY TAKES THE WHEEL

From all around, folks descended on Laguna Beach to see the damage for themselves. Two fender benders were blamed on the lookie-loos.

By Nicole Brodeur
10/31/93

chapter III

ASHES & REBIRTH

N ews choppers, buzzing like gnats around a candle, used tracking antennae and gyro-stabilized cameras to beam back hellish images that would tax Dante's imagination. Thousands of acres flaming: At one point, 14 fires slithered like Spielberg monsters across Southern California. Where would it all end? No one knew.

The basin lay seemingly helpless, a victim of errant air currents, hostage to downed power lines and crazies with matches. Its citizens witnessed tornadoes of fire whirling like Biblical visions, chorus lines of flame doing manic Busby Berkeley routines across ridgelines; clouds on the horizon billowing like steroid-stuffed muscle boys.

As the flames probed through Laguna's canyons, another fire leapt to life in the Ortega forests; citizens wondered: When would the firefighters snap? Had we reached the limits of human endurance?

Then, inexplicably, like an answered prayer the winds died; a wet onshore flow sapped the fire's strength. Firefighters cornered pockets of flame and annihilated them.

After two terrifying days, with 16,682 acres burned, 366 homes and businesses destroyed, 41 others damaged, the Battle of Laguna was won. Miraculously, no lives were lost in the five days of fire.

Now came an enormous outpouring of community spirit. And tears. And hugs. Said one shopkeeper: "How can you say to everyone who's lost everything, 'You have to pay for that toothbrush'?"

Now the survivors trickled back to their moonscape neighborhoods — Skyline, Emerald Bay, El Morro, Temple Hills — and found blankets of ash at one address, eerily untouched houses next door.

Politicians helicoptered in and issued calls for bigger reservoirs, longer arson sentences — but the brutal truth was uttered by Orange County's fire chief: Nothing human could have stopped this fire.

We are, in the end, governed by the ungovernable. By the mysterious ways of the winds. And by the ancient cycle of fire.

LEFT PAGE: WEARY FIREFIGHTERS SLEEP LIKE MUMMIES IN THE DOORWAYS OF LAGUNA'S UPSCALE BUSINESSES.
PHOTO: MICHAEL KITADA

NEXT PAGE: THE FIRES EXHALE VAST BILLOWS OF SMOKE ALONG LAGUNA CANYON ROAD.
PHOTO: CHAS METIVIER

59

OFFICIALS KEY IN ON WHAT WENT WRONG

Firefighters in some burning Laguna Beach neighborhoods had extremely low water pressure for more than six crucial hours because three key reservoirs ran dry due to a power outage, a water-district official said Friday.

Officials also acknowledged that for nearly a decade they have failed to remove brush in Emerald Canyon, even though they determined the area posed a significant fire risk.

By James V. Grimaldi
10/30/93

●

NOT EVERYONE CAME TO OFFER HELP

Police said looters stole about $60,000 in jewelry and tapestries in one of four incidents as residents fled the firestorm. Burglars broke into two homes and stole safes as people fled.

By Marilyn Kalfus
10/31/93

●

"THEIR WHOLE ATTITUDE IS, 'WE'RE NOT USED TO TAKING CHARITY; WE'RE USED TO GIVING IT.'"

Betty Jacobson, a Red Cross nurse

PREVIOUS PAGE: ON SKYLINE DRIVE, DAWN BRINGS BITTER TRUTH. LIFE MUST START ANEW.
PHOTO: MICHAEL KITADA

THIS PAGE: AS THE FIRES RAGE, RICHARD LEAVITT IS OVERCOME WITH EMOTION ON THE ROOF OF A FRIEND'S HOME IN PELICAN COVE.
PHOTO: JIM MAX

PREVIOUS SPREAD: SITTING IN
IMPROBABLE ISOLATION, ONE
HOUSE SURVIVES IN APTLY NAMED
MYSTIC HILLS.
PHOTO: CHAS METIVIER

TOP: MUTE TESTAMENT TO THE
FIRE'S FEROCIOUS ENERGY, A CAR
SITS MELTED TO THE PAVEMENT, ITS
TIRES MELTED DOWN TO THE STEEL
BELTS, PAINT VAPORIZED, INTERIOR
CHARRED.
PHOTO: MICHAEL GOULDING

RIGHT: LAGUNA ANIMAL SERVICES
OFFICER JOY LINGENFELTER MINIS-
TERS TO A STRICKEN DEER. THE
ANIMAL LATER WAS DESTROYED.
PHOTO: BRUCE STRONG

TOP: MARINES DEPLOY TO PROBE THE SMOKING WRECKAGE.

LEFT: NICK HERNANDEZ, ORDINARILY ASSIGNED TO JOHN WAYNE AIRPORT FIRE DUTY, NAPS AT THURSTON SCHOOL.
PHOTOS: BRUCE STRONG

PREVIOUS PAGE: IN A LANDSCAPE AS SURREAL AS ANY POST-APOCALYPTIC BATTLEFIELD, EL TORO MARINES MOVE CAUTIOUSLY THROUGH HOT EMBERS, SEARCHING FOR BODIES. MIRACULOUSLY, THERE WERE NONE.
PHOTO: BRUCE STRONG

TOP: JIM MIPAL BEGINS THE SAD AND DISCOURAGING WORK OF CLEARING HIS RUINED HOUSE.
PHOTO: DANIEL A. ANDERSON

RIGHT: THE ASHES SURRENDER A BATTERED STRONGBOX; ONLY CHARRED PAPERS WERE INSIDE.
PHOTO: NADIA BOROWSKI

FAR RIGHT: THE RUINS OF CARIBBEAN WAY.
PHOTO: BRUCE STRONG

SIFTING THROUGH DISASTER'S RUBBLE

A pot-bellied stove and a view of the coast from Main Beach to Seal Rock.

That and a few other artifacts were all that's left of the four-bedroom, one-story, white stucco house at the end of Coronado Drive.

By Katie Hickox, Susan Kelleher and Chris Boucly
10/29/93

•

GOVERNOR OFFERS HELP AND ADMONITION

Wilson said homeowners were partly to blame for the acceleration of Wednesday's firestorms.

He pointed to homes built up to the edge of steep slopes, brush within 35 feet of the homes and streets too narrow for fire equipment to maneuver.

"It's just too much to ask from the firefighters, asking them to risk their lives needlessly and against the odds."

By Tracy Weber and Jeordan Legon
10/29/93

•

ARMANDE GRIEGER RETURNS TO WHAT IS LEFT OF HER HOME ON IRONICALLY NAMED BOUNTY WAY. **PHOTO: ED CARREON**

TOP: STEPHANIE RACH COMFORTS SISTER LAURIE COOPER AS SHE RECEIVES NEWS THAT HER KITTEN DIDN'T SURVIVE THE EMERALD BAY FIRE THAT ALSO CLAIMED THEIR HOME AND BELONGINGS.
PHOTO: DANIEL A. ANDERSON

FAR RIGHT: IT WASN'T ALL TEARS IN THE RUINS OF LAGUNA. NETTE PATTERSON FINDS A FIGURINE THAT SHE GAVE TO JOAN JARBOE IN JARBOE'S PACIFIC AVENUE HOME. **PHOTO: DAVE YODER**

RIGHT: STRANGELY TRANSFORMED BY THE FLAMES, A STATUE STANDS SENTINEL IN A GARDEN OF ASH.
PHOTO: DANIEL A. ANDERSON

LEFT PAGE: TERI SYFAN (LEFT) AND SALLY FORBES COMFORT ONE ANOTHER AMID THE DEVASTATION OF EMERALD BAY.
PHOTO: MICHAEL GOULDING

LEFT: IN THE DRIVEWAY OF THE HURDLE FAMILY RESIDENCE ON SKYLINE DRIVE, FRIENDS WELCOME THE FAMILY HOME. THEY HAD LIVED THERE A SCANT FIVE MONTHS. **PHOTO: BRUCE STRONG**

TOP: WHERE TO BEGIN RECONSTRUCTING A LIFETIME'S POSSESSIONS? THE QUESTION LEAVES BOB WEST DEEP IN THOUGHT.
PHOTO: NADIA BOROWSKI

A FEW FRAGILE MEMORIES SURVIVED

Martha Lydick held up a teacup amid the charred rubble of her home and teased her husband, federal Judge Lawrence Lydick. "Remember how you always used to say these cups were too delicate?" she asked. Two white, black and gold china cups, along with a few plates and a creamer, were among the few things left in the couple's house.

By Susan Kelleher
10/31/93

DESTRUCTION OF AN ARTIST'S LEGACY

Standing in his back yard Thursday, Peter Paul Ott picked up a pile of plaster of Paris molds for his father's sculptures. Brittle from the heat of the fire, they crumbled in his hands.

"We'll never be able to get this back," Ott murmured. "Gone forever."

By Laura Saari
10/29/93

> "THIS HAS ALWAYS BEEN AN ART COMMUNITY, BECAUSE LAGUNA HAS ALL THAT LIGHT. ALL THAT BEAUTIFUL LIGHT. NOW, EMOTIONALLY, THEY'LL LOOK AT THIS PLACE DIFFERENTLY IN THEIR ART."
>
> Serge Armando,
> Laguna Beach artist

TAKING AN INVENTORY OF TRAGEDY, LISA AHLKE FINDS FRAGILE CROCKERY IMPROBABLY INTACT IN THE RUBBLE.
PHOTO: MICHAEL GOULDING

LEFT: MARGARET AFFHAUSER
APPLIES THE COUP DE GRACE TO A
LINGERING FIRE IN A FRIEND'S
HOME ON PARK AVENUE.
PHOTO: BRUCE STRONG

BOTTOM: ROBERT AHJKLE
LOOKS THROUGH THE RUBBLE OF A
FRIEND'S HOME IN EMERALD BAY.
PHOTO: MICHAEL GOULDING

TOP: A LAGUNA RESIDENT
SEARCHES FOR TREASURES.
PHOTO: DAVE YODER

RIGHT: CHARLES ATWOOD AND
HIS WIFE LIVED MORE THAN 20
YEARS ON TAHITI AVENUE IN
LAGUNA; THEY RETURNED ON THE
FRIDAY AFTER THE FIRESTORM.
PHOTO: BRUCE STRONG

NEXT SPREAD: 'THE FIREMEN
SPOILED US' WITH CHIPS AND
SODA, SAID DUSTIN CARIS, 7, AS
HE TALKED WITH FRIENDS BRET
BURGE, 6, AND STEVE HANSON
OF THE SACRAMENTO FIRE
DEPARTMENT. **PHOTO: BRUCE
STRONG**

LEARNING TO ACCEPT THE FIRE'S REALITY

It is pretty easy to identify the ones who've pretty much accepted their loss. Some of them smile – even laugh. Others have a peaceful, almost thoughtful look about them as they lean on their shovels or shuffle the ashes with their feet, the way third basemen do before a pitch.

By Bill Johnson
11/2/93

NOW THEY NOTICE DEAN BRAUNSTETTER

People used to walk past Dean Braunstetter as he played his guitar on a Laguna Beach street corner.

"People who have seen me every day for years just started talking to me today," said Braunstetter, 42, standing in front of a Salvation Army truck Friday with a few of his homeless friends.

"That's because they have lost everything," said Mason Stone, 22. "Now they know how it feels to be homeless."

By Nicole Brodeur
and Marilyn Kalfus
10/30/93

"IT ALMOST SEEMS LIKE THEY HAVE MORE VOLUNTEERS THAN VICTIMS."
Mary Pat Strauss, of Irvine, church volunteer

SISTERS STEPHANIE AND KIMBERLY RACH OF EMERALD BAY TEND TO THEIR PET.
PHOTO: DANIEL A. ANDERSON

TOP: AN EMERALD BAY WINDOW LOOKS NOWHERE, AT SOMETHING WORSE THAN NOTHING. **PHOTO: MARK AVERY**

RIGHT: GABRIELLE AND JOHN HARWOOD, WHO LOST THEIR CANYON ACRES HOME, JOIN AN ANGRY, CONFUSED CROWD THRONGING THE FIRST LAGUNA BEACH CITY COUNCIL MEETING AFTER THE FIRE, SEARCHING FOR ANSWERS — OR, PERHAPS, VILLAINS. **PHOTO: BRUCE STRONG.**

RIGHT PAGE: JUDY DUROCHER WALKS, ALONE WITH HER THOUGHTS, IN THE RUINS OF CANYON ACRES. **PHOTO: DANIEL A. ANDERSON**

IT BURNED HIS HOUSE; THE TIKI GOD SURVIVED

In the darkness Thursday night, Tom Homan climbed the stairs that used to lead to his house.

In the back yard, Homan's Hawaiian-style pool had survived unscathed. The tiki carvings still hung over the oval-shaped pool and its waterfalls. Using a firefighter's flashlight, Homan found a foot-high mermaid figurine next to the pool.

By Marilyn Kalfus,
10/29/93

"NATURE AND ARSONISTS CONSPIRED TO BRING ABOUT THIS DISASTER. ... AN ARMY OF FIREFIGHTERS COULD NOT HAVE PREVENTED THE DESTRUCTION."
Larry Holms
Orange County fire chief

ONE CHURCH SHOWS THE FIRE'S POWER

At St. Catherine's Catholic Church, whose parish was only blocks away from the path of the flames, Sunday Mass gave the church an opportunity to account for parishioners.

The fire left nearly 60 parish families homeless.

By Venise Wagner
and Mary Ann Milbourn
11/1/93

REX SPRAGGINS OF THE ORANGE COUNTY CHAPLAINS ASSOCIATION CONSOLES KARL DAVISON AS HE INSPECTS THE RUINS OF HIS PARENTS' LAGUNA BEACH HOME.
PHOTO: BRUCE STRONG

FAR LEFT: SHARON HARDY, WHOSE LAGUNA HOME RODE OUT THE FIRE, ATTENDS SERVICES AT LAGUNA PRESBYTERIAN CHURCH. **PHOTO: BRUCE STRONG**

MIDDLE LEFT: ADAM DONNER HELPS UNLOAD CONTRIBUTIONS AT LAGUNA FIRE RELIEF ORGANIZATION HEADQUARTERS. **PHOTO: BRUCE STRONG**

NEAR LEFT: JOHN AND BARBARA LANE, WHOSE HOME BURNED, COPE WITH BUREAUCRATIC FORMS. **PHOTO: DANIEL A. ANDERSON**

BELOW: TONS OF SUPPLIES DESCEND ON THE VILLAGE. **PHOTO: BRUCE STRONG**

SEARCHING FOR HOPE AMID THE DESOLATION

The fire had been so hot that it melted metal.

"There was nothing," said Claes Andersen, co-owner of Hotel Laguna. "I got extremely upset; I thought things were looted."

But there were tiny miracles waiting. Two European clocks that had been in his family for more than 100 years somehow survived; firefighter Ron Rowe hid them in the bushes so they wouldn't be stolen. Rowe called Hotel Laguna to give Andersen the map to his last remaining treasures.

By Teri Sforza
10/31/93

IT'S THE LITTLE THINGS THAT COUNT

One item of clothing was particularly in demand at the Red Cross shelter at Dana Hills High School.

"Most people didn't think about underwear," said Nancy Woloshyn, Red Cross volunteer from Lake Forest.

By Marilyn Kalfus
10/29/93

> **"LAST WEEK WAS HORRIBLE. WE WERE SO STRESSED OUT THAT TODAY WE SAID, 'LET'S JUST PLAY CARDS.'"**
> **Peggy Simkins,**
> **Coto de Caza**

LEFT: SUN SETS ON SKYLINE DRIVE A WEEK AFTER THE FIRESTORMS.
PHOTO: BRUCE STRONG

LAST PAGE: THE LAND LIES NAKED, EXPOSED TO NEW DANGERS: WINTER'S APPROACHING RAINS.
PHOTO: H. LORREN AU JR.

LESSONS LEARNED FROM FIRES PAST

New housing developments on Newport Coast were spared from the fire that ravaged Laguna Beach, partly because of so-called fuel-modification zones. The zones are strips of land that extend from 100 to 1,000 feet from the home. They are usually built in four phases at varying depths. Within each zone existing vegetation is modified or replaced with fire-resistant plants to create a barrier. County and city officials have mandated that such zones be created around homes that back into chaparral, parks or forests. And most major developments built in the county in the past 10 to 15 years contain them. Here's how a 250-foot fuel-modification zone would work and how homeowners can benefit from the technique.

NEWPORT COAST

ORANGE COUNTY

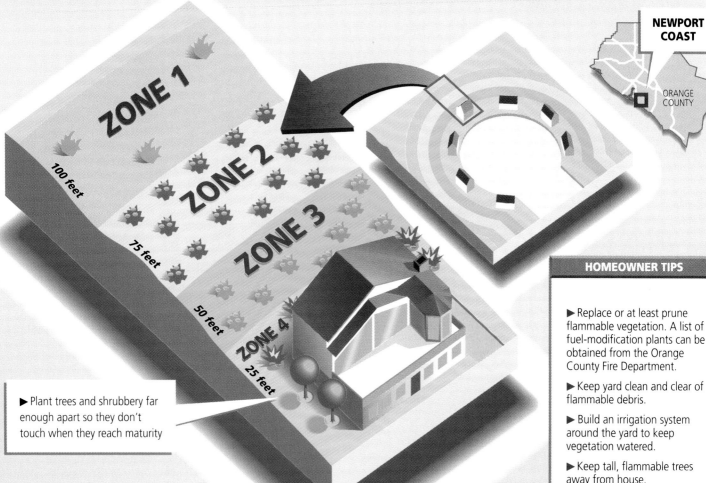

ZONE 1
100 feet
ZONE 2
75 feet
ZONE 3
50 feet
ZONE 4
25 feet

► Plant trees and shrubbery far enough apart so they don't touch when they reach maturity

HOMEOWNER TIPS

► Replace or at least prune flammable vegetation. A list of fuel-modification plants can be obtained from the Orange County Fire Department.

► Keep yard clean and clear of flammable debris.

► Build an irrigation system around the yard to keep vegetation watered.

► Keep tall, flammable trees away from house.

► If property is large enough, build a fuel-modification zone. Landscape architects typically charge $75 to consult. Building the zone can run well above $1,000.

► Maintain vegetation around house. Even fuel-modification zones become ineffective when they are not tended.

► Avoid pine, eucalyptus and cedar trees, which are highly flammable.

► Use ice plant, myoporum and Aaron's beard, which are fire-resistant.

ZONE 1: Existing vegetation is thinned out to reduce potential fire fuel. If extremely flammable plants such as buckwheat, sagebrush or chamise exist, they are removed.

SAGEBRUSH

ZONE 2: Drought-tolerant and low-lying, fire-resistant plants such as yarrow, salvias or California poppy are seeded or planted. An irrigation system is sometimes installed.

YARROW

ZONE 3: Another layer of fire-resistant plants such as salt-bushes, rock roses or santolina is planted to make an aesthetic transition between the natural landscape and the back yard.

SANTOLINA

ZONE 4: The last zone, often called the wet zone, is constructed with fire-retardant vegetation such as ice plants, cape weeds and coyote plants. This zone also contains the yard.

ICE PLANTS

Graphics reporting: KELLY BARRON

Source: Waldo Dale Landscape Architecture, Edaw Inc., County of Orange.

GEORGE TURNEY and JAMES ZISK
The Orange County Register

STOPPING A BRUSH FIRE

Protected home: As fire's 20-foot-high flames approach, irrigated fire-resistant plants and zones of thinned vegetation deprive the fire of fuel, slowing it and eventually stopping it. Houses set back from the hill's edge give firefighters room to work.

Unprotected home: Tall, dry brush on the hillside is super-heated by the 20-foot-high flames at the hill's base. Flames race up the hill, gathering strength. With no room for firefighters to work, the home can not survive a brush fire.

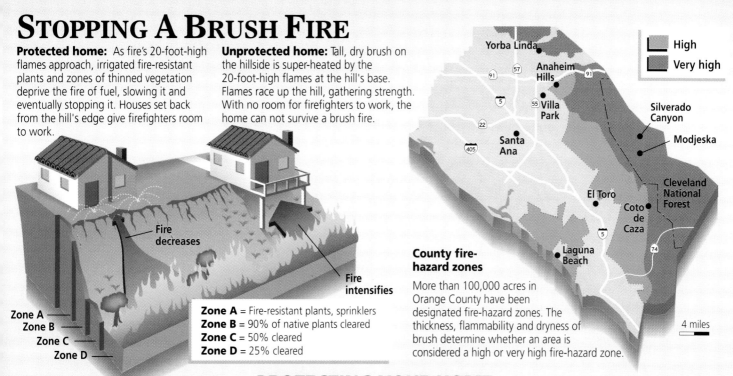

Fire decreases

Fire intensifies

Zone A
Zone B
Zone C
Zone D

Zone A = Fire-resistant plants, sprinklers
Zone B = 90% of native plants cleared
Zone C = 50% cleared
Zone D = 25% cleared

High
Very high

Yorba Linda
Anaheim Hills
Villa Park
Santa Ana
Silverado Canyon
Modjeska
El Toro
Coto de Caza
Cleveland National Forest
Laguna Beach

4 miles

County fire-hazard zones

More than 100,000 acres in Orange County have been designated fire-hazard zones. The thickness, flammability and dryness of brush determine whether an area is considered a high or very high fire-hazard zone.

PROTECTING YOUR HOME

Nothing a firefighter can do will protect your home if you have not prepared for fire. The Orange County Fire Department urges you to create a defensible space around your home by using fire-safe landscaping and taking other safety precautions.

BEFORE THE FIRE

1. Clear all flammable vegetation a minimum of 50 feet around the house.

2. Grow fire-resistant plants in a zone 50 to 100 feet from the house. Plant vegetation that grows close to the ground, has low sap or resin content, grows without accumulating dead leaves and is easily maintained.

3. Clean up and clear the area 100 to 150 feet from your house. Thin living brush and clear away dead vegetation.

4. Put liquid petroleum gas (LPG) tanks and any fuel containers at least 30 feet from the house. Clear 10 feet around all tanks.

5. Roof with fire-resistant materials.

6. Cover attic and other vents.

7. Never allow rubbish to pile up near house or garage.

8. Establish emergency water supply of at least 2,500 gallons. Water can come from a well, below-ground storage tanks, swimming pools or streams. Have a gasoline-powered generator or pump on hand to move water during power loss.

For more information on wildfire safety, call your fire department or write the California Department of Forestry, Southern Region, 2524 Mulberry St., Riverside, Calif. 92501.

WHEN FIRE THREATENS

When an evacuation order seems imminent, there are steps you can take to protect your family and property. If there is time:

9. Dress properly. Wear long pants and long-sleeved shirts.

10. Disconnect automatic garage doors, close the door, leave it unlocked.

11. Park car in garage, heading out, with windows rolled up and keys in ignition. Place valuable documents, family mementos and pets in the car.

12. Move lawn furniture away from house.

13. Attach garden hoses to spigots.

14. Fill trash cans and buckets with water where firefighters can find them.

15. Prepare emergency generators and pumps; leave instructions for firefighters.

16. Place a ladder against your house on the side opposite approaching fire.

17. Place a lawn sprinkler on roof, but don't turn it on.

18. Turn on all lights to make house easy to find in smoke.

Graphic: George Turney

Source: OC Fire Dept. Office of Hazard Reduction